NATURAL BISCUITS

Original and appealing recipes for a variety
of home-baked wholefood biscuits.

In the same series
NATURAL PÂTÉS
NATURAL SPICES
NATURAL SWEETS

By the same author
FRESH FRUIT COCKTAILS
THE CAROB COOKBOOK

NATURAL BISCUITS

by

Lorraine Whiteside

Illustrated by Clive Birch

THORSONS PUBLISHERS LIMITED
Wellingborough, Northamptonshire

First published 1984

British Library Cataloguing in Publication Data

Whiteside, Lorraine
    Natural biscuits.
    1. Crackers   2. Cookies   3. Cookery
    I. Title
    641.8'654   TX769

    ISBN 0-7225-0915-4

Reproduced, printed and bound in Great Britain by
Hazell Watson & Viney Limited,
Member of the BPCC Group,
Aylesbury, Bucks

CONTENTS

INTRODUCTION

Biscuits made at home with all natural ingredients have a unique appeal that simply cannot be matched by machine-made biscuits. The delicious flavour and welcoming aroma of home-made biscuits are evocative of one's childhood days, when home-baking was an integral part of daily life, a tradition that sadly has been overtaken by the appearance of readily available convenience foods.

Traditions may well change, but the need to feed our bodies with maximum nourishment never alters. And therein, I think, lies the greatest appeal of home-made, wholemeal biscuits — the knowledge that they are made with only the very best natural ingredients, with all the goodness that nature intended us to have, with none of the refined elements and unnatural additives found in so many shop-bought varieties.

Nutrition aside, there is a sheer joy in making one's own biscuits, for not only are they simple to make, they also have a happy habit of always turning out well. And let's not forget that although health food stores stock a good range of wholemeal biscuits, they tend to be very pricey, and therefore the economical advantages of home-baked biscuits are great.

Moreover, we are becoming increasingly aware, as a nation, of the value of dietary fibre for the maintenance of good health, and often it is our so-called snack foods that are lacking in fibre. With wholemeal biscuits, however, you can be sure that you and your family are enjoying a snack that is both nourishing and high in fibre.

I hope that you enjoy making these biscuits as much as I enjoyed testing them for this book. I feel sure that you will be faced with the same problem that I always have when making wholemeal biscuits — I simply cannot make them quickly enough for my family!

TYPES OF BISCUITS

ROLLED BISCUITS

These are biscuits that are made from a fairly stiff dough that is rolled out on a floured board and cut into shapes. If you find that the dough is slightly soft or sticky, knead in a little extra flour to give it added firmness. There is no need to keep to the conventional round-shaped biscuit cutter — diamonds, stars and hearts make pretty alternatives.

DROP BISCUITS

These are made from a softer dough that is spooned directly onto the baking sheet and formed into neat circles or fingers by levelling and shaping with the teaspoon. Alternatively, the dough can be rolled into small balls with the hands, then compressed on the baking sheet with the palm of the hand. Always leave plenty of space between drop biscuits, as they will spread whilst baking, particularly if the dough is very soft.

TRAY BISCUITS AND BAKES

These are baked in a Swiss-roll tin or shallow baking tin, then cut into shapes after baking. Some of the recipes in this section are not strictly biscuit recipes, and this is why I like to call them 'bakes', for they are in between a biscuit and a small cake. Tray biscuits and bakes are my own favourites because they allow plenty of scope for creativity and experimentation with different flavours and combinations, giving delicious results every time.

INGREDIENTS

Wholemeal Flour — contains one hundred per cent of the wheat grain, with the germ and bran naturally present. Wholemeal flour is an important source of dietary fibre and of vitamins E and B.

Polyunsaturated Margarine — soft margarine of vegetable origin, high in polyunsaturates, low in cholesterol.

Raw Cane Sugar — natural product of the sugar cane, containing varying degrees of molasses. Nutritively more acceptable than highly refined white sugar. Raw Demerara and light Muscovado sugars are best for biscuit-making. Look for the country of origin on the pack to make sure that it is genuine raw cane sugar.

Dried Fruits — concentrated sources of natural fruit sugars, rich in essential vitamins and minerals. Experiment with some of the delicious exotic varieties, such as pineapple and papaya, now widely available in health food stores.

Nuts — important source of vegetable protein, with a high

energy value, adding flavour and essential nutrients to wholemeal biscuits.

Honey — one of nature's purest natural sugars, easily assimilated by the body and rapidly converted into energy. Honey contains essential vitamins and minerals and is renowned for its curative properties. Honey flavours and enriches wholemeal biscuits.

Natural Yogurt — rich in protein, calcium and the B vitamins, with a low fat content. Natural yogurt is ideal for binding dry ingredients together when making biscuits, scones and cakes, as a low-cholesterol alternative to eggs.

Molasses — highly concentrated source of vitamins and minerals, made up of the nutritive residue resulting from the cane sugar refining process. Its distinctive flavour blends well with ginger, cinnamon and mixed spices.

Carob — natural alternative to chocolate and cocoa powder, containing neither of the stimulants, caffeine and theobromine, present in the cocoa bean.

Leavening Agent — the leavening agent used throughout the book is bicarbonate of soda. This is an alkaline substance which is used in conjunction with an acid substance such as natural yogurt, molasses, honey, soured cream, buttermilk, citrus juice or cream of tartar. It is the combination of alkaline and acid substances that activates the leavening process.

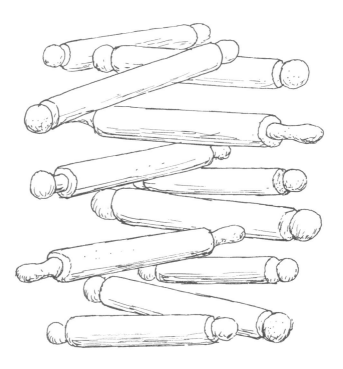

ROLLED BISCUITS

CURRANT BISCUITS

4 oz (115g) polyunsaturated margarine
3 oz (85g) raw cane sugar
2 teaspoonsful clear honey
Finely grated zest of 1 orange
1 egg, lightly beaten
2 oz (55g) currants
½ lb (225g) wholemeal flour
¼ level teaspoonful bicarbonate of soda
Lightly beaten egg white, to glaze

1. Cream the margarine, raw cane sugar, honey and finely grated orange zest together until soft and fluffy.

2. Gradually incorporate the egg, beating well.

3. Add the currants, then fold in the wholemeal flour and bicarbonate of soda, mixing well to obtain a fairly stiff consistency.

4. Roll the mixture out on a lightly floured board and cut into rounds with a fluted biscuit cutter. Place the biscuits on greased baking sheets and brush all over with lightly beaten egg white, to glaze.

5. Bake at 350°F/180°C (Gas Mark 4) for about 15 minutes, until lightly browned and firm to the touch.

Makes about 30 biscuits.

PINEAPPLE AND ORANGE BISCUITS

Natural dried pineapple is combined with fresh orange juice, ground almonds and other natural ingredients to make these delicious and nutritious biscuits.

4 oz (115g) polyunsaturated margarine
3 oz (85g) raw cane sugar
2 teaspoonsful clear honey
Finely grated zest of 1 orange
1 egg yolk
2 fl oz (50ml) fresh orange juice
4 oz (115g) dried pineapple, finely diced
5 oz (140g) wholemeal flour
¼ level teaspoonful bicarbonate of soda
4 oz (115g) ground almonds
Lightly beaten egg white, to glaze

For decoration

About 30 small pieces dried pineapple
Clear honey

1. Cream the margarine, sugar, clear honey and finely grated orange zest together until soft and fluffy.

2. Incorporate the egg yolk, beating well, then gradually incorporate the fresh orange juice.

3. Add the finely diced dried pineapple, then fold in the wholemeal flour, bicarbonate of soda and ground almonds, mixing well to obtain a fairly stiff consistency.

4.   Roll the mixture out on a lightly floured board and cut into rounds with a fluted biscuit cutter. Place on greased baking sheets and brush all over with lightly beaten egg white.

5.   Bake the biscuits at 350°F/180°C (Gas Mark 4) for about 15 minutes, until lightly browned and firm to the touch.

6.   Allow the biscuits to cool thoroughly, then decorate with small pieces of dried pineapple, secured with a little clear honey.

Makes about 30 biscuits.

BRAN AND RAISIN BISCUITS

Delicious fibre-rich biscuits, with a hint of cinnamon.

4 oz (115g) polyunsaturated margarine
3 oz (85g) light Muscovado sugar
2 teaspoonsful clear honey
1 egg, lightly beaten
2 oz (55g) small raisins, finely diced
6 oz (170g) wholemeal flour
2 oz (55g) bran plus (wheat bran with the germ
  naturally present)
1½ level teaspoonsful ground cinnamon
¼ level teaspoonful bicarbonate of soda
Lightly beaten egg white, to glaze

1. Cream the margarine, Muscovado sugar and honey together until soft and fluffy.

2. Gradually incorporate the egg, beating well, then fold in the diced raisins.

3. Mix together the wholemeal flour, bran plus, cinnamon and bicarbonate of soda, then fold into the mixture, mixing well to give a fairly stiff consistency.

4. Roll out on a lightly floured board and cut into rounds with a fluted biscuit cutter.

5. Place the biscuits on greased baking sheets and brush all over with lightly beaten egg white.

6. Bake at 350°F/180°C (Gas Mark 4) for about 15 minutes, until firm to the touch.

Bran and Sultana Biscuits: Prepare the biscuits by the same method as above, using 2 oz (55g) of finely diced sultanas in place of the raisins.

Makes about 30 biscuits.

APRICOT AND PAPAYA SQUARES

The flavour and goodness of two delicious dried fruits are combined with almonds and other natural ingredients to make these unusually tasty biscuits.

4 oz (115g) dried apricots
6 fl oz (175ml) pure orange juice
2 unblanched Jordan almonds
4 oz (115g) polyunsaturated margarine
3 oz (85g) raw cane sugar
2 teaspoonsful clear honey
4 oz (115g) dried papaya, finely diced
1 oz (30g) flaked almonds, crumbled
½ lb (225g) wholemeal flour
¼ level teaspoonful bicarbonate of soda
2 oz (55g) ground almonds
About 28 split blanched almonds
Lightly beaten egg white, to glaze

1. Cover the dried apricots with the orange juice. Split the unblanched almonds in half and add to the apricots and orange juice. Cover and leave to soak overnight. (The almonds will add a subtle flavour to the soaking juice.)

2. After the soaking period, discard the almonds, then place the apricots and orange juice in a blender and blend to a smooth, thick purée.

3. Cream the margarine, raw cane sugar and honey

together until soft and fluffy. Add the apricot and orange purée, beating well.

4. Reserve about one tablespoonful of the diced papaya for decoration, then add the remainder to the creamed apricot mixture, together with the crumbled flaked almonds. Now fold in the flour, bicarbonate of soda and ground almonds, mixing well to obtain a fairly stiff consistency.

5. Roll the mixture out on a lightly floured board and cut out with a square-shaped biscuit cutter. Place the biscuits on greased baking sheets and press a split blanched almond into the centre of each one.

6. Brush the biscuits all over with lightly beaten egg white, then bake at 350°F/180°C (Gas Mark 4) for about 15 minutes, until lightly browned.

7. Before serving the biscuits, sprinkle a little of the reserved papaya over each one, for decoration.

Makes about 28 squares.

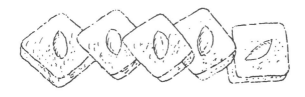

LANCASHIRE CHEESE BISCUITS

A fine English cheese is combined with oatmeal and other natural ingredients to make these tasty savoury biscuits.

> 6 oz (170g) wholemeal flour
> 2 oz (55g) medium oatmeal
> ¼ level teaspoonful bicarbonate of soda
> ½ teaspoonful sea salt
> ½ level teaspoonful paprika
> 2 twists freshly milled black pepper
> 3 oz (85g) polyunsaturated margarine
> 4 oz (115g) mature Lancashire cheese, grated
> 1 egg, lightly beaten
> 1-2 tablespoonsful milk
> Lightly beaten egg white, to glaze
> Poppy seeds or sesame seeds

1. Combine the wholemeal flour, oatmeal, bicarbonate of soda, sea salt, paprika and black pepper in a mixing bowl.

2. Rub the margarine into the dry ingredients, until the mixture resembles fine breadcrumbs. Fold in the grated Lancashire cheese.

3. Now incorporate the beaten egg, together with sufficient milk to bind the ingredients to a stiff, workable dough.

4. Roll the mixture out on a lightly floured board and

cut into rounds with a plain biscuit cutter. Place on greased baking sheets and brush all over with lightly beaten egg white. Now sprinkle the biscuits with poppy seeds or sesame seeds.

5. Bake at 350°F/180°C (Gas Mark 4) for 15-20 minutes, until lightly browned and firm to the touch.

Makes about 24 biscuits.

Note: Prepare the biscuits as above, using your own regional cheese, in place of Lancashire.

ALMOND BISCUITS

6 oz (170g) wholemeal flour
2 oz (55g) ground almonds
3 oz (85g) raw cane sugar
¼ level teaspoonful bicarbonate of soda
½ teaspoonful almond essence
5 oz (140g) polyunsaturated margarine
1 teaspoonful clear honey
About 60 split blanched almonds
Lightly beaten egg white, to glaze

1. Combine the wholemeal flour, ground almonds, raw cane sugar, bicarbonate of soda and almond essence in a mixing bowl.

2. Using the fingertips, rub the margarine into the dry ingredients, then incorporate the clear honey and knead the mixture to a stiff dough.

3. Roll out on a lightly floured board and cut into rounds with a fluted biscuit cutter.

4. Place the biscuits on greased baking sheets and press two split blanched almonds into the centre of each one.

5. Brush the biscuits with lightly beaten egg white, then bake at 350°F/180°C (Gas Mark 4) for about 15 minutes, until golden brown.

Makes about 30 biscuits.

OATCAKES

High in protein and rich in fibre, oatcakes are a traditional Scottish breakfast food, delicious spread with honey or served with cheese.

6 oz (170g) medium oatmeal
2 oz (55g) wholemeal flour
¼ teaspoonful sea salt
¼ level teaspoonful bicarbonate of soda
1½ oz (40g) polyunsaturated margarine
1 teaspoonful honey
Boiling water to mix

1. Combine the oatmeal, wholemeal flour, sea salt and bicarbonate of soda in a mixing bowl.

2. Melt the margarine and honey together in a saucepan set over a moderate heat.

3. Add the melted margarine and honey to the dry ingredients, together with sufficient boiling water to bind the mixture to a stiff, workable dough.

4. Turn the mixture out onto a board that has been lightly floured with fine oatmeal, and roll out as thinly as possible. Cut into rounds with a plain biscuit cutter, or cut into triangles, using a floured knife.

5. Place the oatcakes on greased baking sheets and bake at 350°F/180°C (Gas Mark 4) for 15-20 minutes, until lightly browned.

Makes about 24 oatcakes.

CAROB COATED ORANGE BISCUITS

These orange zest-flavoured biscuits are completed with a dark, orange-flavoured carob coating.

4 oz (115g) polyunsaturated margarine
3 oz (85g) raw cane sugar
2 teaspoonsful clear honey
Finely grated zest of 1 orange
1 egg, lightly beaten
½ lb (225g) wholemeal flour
¼ level teaspoonful bicarbonate of soda
Lightly beaten egg white, to glaze

For the carob coating:

One 2.8 oz (80g) orange-flavoured carob bar

1. Cream the margarine, raw cane sugar, honey and finely grated orange zest together until soft and fluffy.

2. Gradually incororate the egg, beating well.

3. Now fold in the wholemeal flour and bicarbonate of soda, mixing well to obtain a fairly stiff consistency.

4. Roll the mixture out on a lightly floured board and cut into rounds with a fluted biscuit cutter. Place the biscuits on greased baking sheets and brush all over with lightly beaten egg white.

5. Bake at 350°F/180°C (Gas Mark 4) for about 15 minutes, until golden brown.

6. To make the coating, break the carob bar into pieces and place in a heat-resistant basin. Stand the basin in a saucepan of hot water, until the carob is smooth and thoroughly melted.

7. Spread the orange-flavoured carob coating over the underside of the biscuits and leave to set.

Makes about 30 biscuits.

CLIVE BIRCH

CHRISTMAS FRUIT AND NUT BISCUITS

I have named these dried fruit and almond laden biscuits 'Christmas' biscuits, because they are flavoured with the juice and grated zest of a mandarin orange, that delicious little fruit so abundantly available at Christmas time.

½ lb (225g) wholemeal flour
2 oz (55g) ground almonds
¼ level teaspoonful bicarbonate of soda
4 oz (115g) polyunsaturated margarine
4 oz (115g) raw cane sugar
1 oz (30g) dried apricots, finely diced
1 oz (30g) sultanas, finely diced
1 oz (30g) small raisins, finely diced
Finely grated zest of 1 mandarin orange
1 egg, lightly beaten
Strained juice of 1 mandarin orange
About 34 split blanched almonds
Lightly beaten egg white, to glaze

1. Place the wholemeal flour, ground almonds and bicarbonate of soda in a mixing bowl.

2. Rub the margarine into the dry ingredients, until the mixture resembles fine breadcrumbs.

3. Stir in the raw cane sugar, apricots, sultanas, raisins and grated mandarin orange zest.

4. Now incorporate the beaten egg, together with

26

sufficient mandarin orange juice to bind the ingredients to a stiff, workable dough.

5. Roll the mixture out on a lightly floured board and cut into rounds with a fluted biscuit cutter. Press a split blanched almond into the centre of each biscuit, then brush all over with lightly beaten egg white, to glaze.

6. Bake at 350°F/180°C (Gas Mark 4) for about 15 minutes, until golden brown and firm to the touch.

Makes about 34 biscuits.

MOLASSES GINGER NUTS

So easy to make, these delicious little biscuits are laden with flavour.

½ lb (225g) wholemeal flour
1 level teaspoonful ground ginger
½ level teaspoonful ground cinnamon
½ level teaspoonful ground nutmeg
¼ level teaspoonful bicarbonate of soda
4 oz (115g) polyunsaturated margarine
3 oz (85g) light Muscovado sugar
1 level tablespoonful blackstrap molasses
1-2 tablespoonsful natural yogurt
Lightly beaten egg white, to glaze

1. Combine the wholemeal flour, spices and bicarbonate of soda in a mixing bowl.

2. Rub the margarine into the dry ingredients, until the mixture resembles fine breadcrumbs. Now stir in the Muscovado sugar.

3. Melt the molasses in a saucepan set over a moderate heat, then add to the flour mixture, together with sufficient natural yogurt to bind the ingredients to a fairly stiff, workable dough.

4. Roll out on a lightly floured board and cut into circles with a plain biscuit cutter. Place on greased baking sheets and brush all over with lightly beaten egg white.

5. Bake the biscuits at 350°F/180°C (Gas Mark 4) for about 15 minutes, until firm to the touch

Makes about 30 biscuits.

APRICOT AND CASHEW NUT BISCUITS

Fruity and nutty, made with dried apricots, cashew nuts, ground almonds and other natural ingredients.

4 oz (115g) polyunsaturated margarine
3 oz (85g) raw cane sugar
2 teaspoonsful clear honey
Finely grated zest of 1 orange
1 egg, lightly beaten
2 oz (55g) dried apricots, finely diced
2 oz (55g) cashew nuts, finely diced
6 oz (170g) wholemeal flour
¼ level teaspoonful bicarbonate of soda
2 oz (55g) ground almonds
About 30 halved cashew nuts
Lightly beaten egg white, to glaze

1. Cream the margarine, raw cane sugar, honey and finely grated orange zest together until soft and fluffy.

2. Gradually incorporate the egg, beating well.

3. Now add the finely diced apricots and cashew nuts, then fold in the wholemeal flour, bicarbonate of soda and ground almonds, mixing well to obtain a fairly stiff consistency.

4. Roll the mixture out on a lightly floured board and cut into rounds with a fluted biscuit cutter. Place on greased baking sheets and press a halved cashew nut into the centre of each biscuit.

5. Brush all over with lightly beaten egg white, then bake at 350°F/180°C (Gas Mark 4) for about 15 minutes, until golden brown and firm to the touch.

Makes about 30 biscuits.

DROP BISCUITS

SUNFLOWER SEED
AND HONEY BISCUITS

Simply delicious protein-rich biscuits, sweetened with honey.

½ lb (255g) wholemeal flour
¼ level teaspoonful bicarbonate of soda
2 oz (55g) light Muscovado sugar
4 oz (115g) sunflower seeds
1 egg, lightly beaten
½ teaspoonful vanilla essence
3 oz (85g) polyunsaturated margarine
2 tablespoonsful honey
Lightly beaten egg white, to glaze

1. Place the wholemeal flour, bicarbonate of soda, Muscovado sugar and sunflower seeds in a mixing bowl.

2. Add the beaten egg and vanilla essence to the dry ingredients.

3. Melt the margarine and honey together in a saucepan set over a moderate heat. When melted, add to the flour mixture, blending well to bind all the ingredients together.

4. Using the hands, take small portions of the mixture and roll into little balls. Place on greased baking sheets and flatten with the palm of the hand, so that you have neat, flat circle shapes. Space the biscuits fairly well apart, to allow room for spreading whilst baking.

5. Brush all over with lightly beaten egg white, then bake at 350°F/180°C (Gas Mark 4) for about 15 minutes, until lightly browned.

Note: For a slightly different flavour, prepare the biscuits with pre-roasted sunflower seeds.

Makes about 30 biscuits.

APRICOT AND ALMOND LOGS

Dried apricots, orange juice and almonds are the basic ingredients that are combined to make these delicious log-shaped biscuits.

4 oz (115g) dried apricots
6 fl oz (175ml) pure orange juice
2 unblanched Jordan almonds
4 oz (115g) polyunsaturated margarine
4 oz (115g) raw cane sugar
½ lb (225g) wholemeal flour
2 oz (55g) ground almonds
¼ level teaspoonful bicarbonate of soda
Lightly beaten egg white
3 oz (85g) flaked almonds, crumbled

1. Cover the dried apricots with the orange juice. Split the unblanched almonds in half and add to the apricots and orange juice. Cover and leave to soak overnight. (The almonds will add a subtle flavour to the soaking juice.)

2. After the soaking period, discard the almonds, then place the apricots and orange juice in a blender and blend to a smooth, thick purée.

3. Cream the margarine and raw cane sugar together until soft and fluffy. Now add the apricot purée, beating well, then fold in the flour, ground almonds and bicarbonate of soda.

4.   Using the hands, take small portions of the mixture and roll into neat log shapes. Brush the logs all over with lightly beaten egg white, then toss in flaked almonds.

5.   Place the logs on greased baking sheets and bake at 350°F/180°C (Gas Mark 4) for 15-20 minutes, until lightly browned.

Makes about 24 logs.

ORANGE MACAROONS

These delectable macaroons contain a subtle hint of orange flavour.

2 egg whites
4 oz (115g) ground almonds
4 oz (115g) light Muscovado sugar
Finely grated zest of 2 oranges
Rice paper
About 32 split blanched almonds

1. Whisk the egg whites until they stand in stiff peaks.

2. Fold in the ground almonds, light Muscovado sugar and grated orange zest, mixing thoroughly until smooth.

3. Spoon or pipe teaspoonsful of the mixture onto baking sheets lined with rice paper. Space the mixture well apart to allow room for the biscuits to spread whilst baking.

4. Decorate each macaroon with one or two split blanched almonds.

5. Bake at 350°F/180°C (Gas Mark 4) for about 15 minutes, until golden brown. Allow the macaroons to cool, then trim off the excess rice paper.

Makes about 16.

LEMON AND HONEY BISCUITS

Honey-sweetened crunchy biscuits, flavoured with freshly grated lemon zest.

4 oz (115g) polyunsaturated margarine
1 oz (30g) raw cane sugar
2 tablespoonsful clear honey
Finely grated zest of 1 lemon
1 egg yolk
5 oz (140g) wholemeal flour
¼ level teaspoonful bicarbonate of soda
1 oz (30g) fine oatmeal

1. Cream the margarine, raw cane sugar, honey and lemon zest together until smooth and creamy.

2. Incorporate the egg yolk, beating well.

3. Now fold in the wholemeal flour, bicarbonate of soda and oatmeal, mixing well to a fairly soft dough.

4. Drop teaspoonful of the mixture onto greased baking sheets, smoothing over with the back of the teaspoon and forming into neat circles. Space the mixture well apart to allow room for the biscuits to spread whilst baking.

5. Bake at 350°F/180°C (Gas Mark 4) for about 15 minutes, until golden brown.

Makes about 24 biscuits.

CAROB COATED FRUIT AND NUT FINGERS

A dark carob coating adds the finishing touch to these flavourful fingers, full of the goodness of dried fruits, nuts, molasses, oats and other natural ingredients.

4 oz (115g) polyunsaturated margarine
4 oz (115g) raw cane sugar
1 teaspoonful blackstrap molasses
1 egg, lightly beaten
1 oz (30g) nibbed almonds
1 oz (30g) hazelnuts, finely diced
1 oz (30g) small raisins, finely diced
1 oz (30g) sultanas, finely diced
6 oz (170g) wholemeal flour
1 oz (30g) medium oatmeal
¼ level teaspoonful bicarbonate of soda
Lightly beaten egg white, to glaze

For the carob coating:

One 2.8 oz (80g) plain carob bar

1. Cream the margarine, raw cane sugar and molasses together until soft and fluffy.

2. Gradually incorporate the egg, beating well.

3. Add the nibbed almonds, hazelnuts, raisins and sultanas, then fold in the wholemeal flour, oatmeal and bicarbonate of soda, mixing well to a fairly stiff consistency.

4. Drop heaped teaspoonful of the mixture onto greased baking sheets and form into neat finger shapes. Allow some space between the fingers as they will spread slightly whilst baking.

5. Brush the fingers all over with lightly beaten egg white, then bake at 350°F/180°C (Gas Mark 4) for about 15 minutes, until lightly browned and firm to the touch.

6. To make the coating, break the carob bar into pieces and place in a heat-resistant basin. Stand the basin in a saucepan of hot water, until the carob is smooth and thoroughly melted.

7. Spread the carob coating over the underside of the fingers and leave to set.

Makes about 30 fingers.

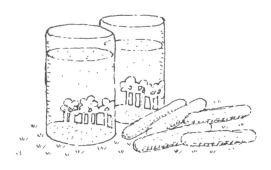

PECAN KISSES

These deliciously nutty biscuits are similar to macaroons, but contain the added goodness of oatmeal.

2 egg whites
4 oz (115g) light Muscovado sugar
3 oz (85g) fine oatmeal
½ teaspoonful vanilla essence
¼ teaspoonful sea salt
4 oz (115g) chopped pecans
Rice paper

1. Whisk the egg whites until they stand in stiff peaks.

2. Fold in the light Muscovado sugar, oatmeal, vanilla essence and sea salt, blending all the ingredients together well. Lastly fold in the chopped pecans.

3. Drop teaspoonful of the mixture onto baking sheets lined with rice paper. Space the mixture well apart to allow room for the biscuits to spread whilst in the oven.

4. Bake at 350°F/180°C (Gas Mark 4) for 15-20 minutes, until lightly browned. Allow the biscuits to cool, then trim off the excess rice paper.

Makes about 16.

WALNUT KISSES

Prepare the biscuit mixture by the method opposite, using chopped walnuts in place of pecans.

love
clare
X

CLIVE
BIRCH

PAPAYA AND ALMOND FINGERS

Tasty wholewheat fingers containing dried papaya and flaked almonds, flavoured with freshly grated orange zest.

> 4 oz (115g) polyunsaturated margarine
> 3 oz (85g) raw cane sugar
> 2 teaspoonsful clear honey
> Finely grated zest of 1 orange
> 1 egg, lightly beaten
> 2 oz (55g) dried papaya, finely diced
> 2 oz (55g) flaked almonds, crumbled
> 7 oz (200g) wholemeal flour
> ¼ level teaspoonful bicarbonate of soda
> Lightly beaten egg white, to glaze

For decoration:

> Small pieces of dried papaya
> Clear honey

1. Cream the margarine, raw cane sugar, honey and grated orange zest together until soft and fluffy.

2. Gradually incorporate the egg, beating well.

3. Add the dried papaya and flaked almonds, then fold in the wholemeal flour and bicarbonate of soda, mixing all the ingredients together well.

4. Place heaped teaspoonsful of the mixture onto greased baking sheets and form into neat finger

42

shapes. Allow some space between the fingers as they will spread slightly whilst baking.

5. Brush the fingers all over with lightly beaten egg white, then bake at 350°F/180°C (Gas Mark 4) for about 15 minutes, until golden brown.

6. When the biscuits have thoroughly cooled, decorate them with small pieces of dried papaya, secured on top of the fingers with a little clear honey.

Makes about 28 fingers.

PINEAPPLE AND ALMOND FINGERS

Prepare and bake the biscuit mixture by the same method as above, using 2 oz (55g) of finely diced dried pineapple in place of the papaya.

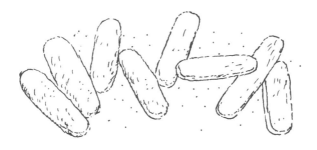

CAROB AND PECAN CRUNCHIES

These biscuits are dark, crunchy and very nutty.

4 oz (115g) polyunsaturated margarine
3 oz (85g) light Muscovado sugar
2 teaspoonsful clear honey
½ teaspoonful vanilla essence
1 egg, lightly beaten
6 oz (170g) chopped pecans
6 oz (170g) wholemeal flour
¼ level teaspoonful bicarbonate of soda
1 oz (30g) carob powder

1. Cream the margarine, Muscovado sugar, honey and vanilla essence together until soft and fluffy.

2. Gradually add the egg, beating well.

3. Incorporate the chopped pecans, then fold in the wholemeal flour, bicarbonate of soda and carob powder, mixing well.

4. Drop teaspoonsful of the mixture onto greased baking sheets, smoothing over with the back of a teaspoon and shaping into neat circles. Space the mixture well apart to allow room for the biscuits to spread whilst baking.

5. Bake at 350°F/180°C (Gas Mark 4) for about 15 minutes, until firm to the touch.

Makes about 36 small biscuits.

ORANGE AND ALMOND PETITS FOURS

These flavour-rich little biscuits are ideal for serving as an after-dinner treat.

2 egg whites
6 oz (170g) ground almonds
3 oz (85g) light Muscovado sugar
Finely grated zest of 1 orange
Rice paper

For decoration:

1 oz (30g) nibbed almonds

1. Whisk the egg whites until they stand in stiff peaks.

2. Fold in the ground almonds, Muscovado sugar and grated orange zest, blending well until smooth.

3. Spoon the mixture into a piping bag fitted with a large star nozzle and pipe 'S' shapes, swirls and finger shapes onto baking sheets lined with rice paper.

4. Decorate the petits fours by dotting with nibbed almonds.

5. Bake at 350°F/180°C (Gas Mark 4) for 12-15 minutes, until lightly browned.

6. Allow the petits fours to cool on the baking sheet, then trim off the excess rice paper.

TRAY BISCUITS AND BAKES

TROPICAL OAT CRUNCH BARS

A taste of the tropics is contained in these crunchy oat bars.

6 oz (170g) rolled oats
1 oz (30g) fine oatmeal
2 oz (55g) wheatgerm
¼ teaspoonful sea salt
2 oz (55g) dried pineapple, finely diced
1 oz (30g) dried papaya, finely diced
½ oz (15g) coconut flakes
1½ oz (40g) dried banana chips, crumbled
1 oz (30g) ground almonds
3 oz (85g) flaked almonds
2 oz (55g) raw cane sugar
3 tablespoonsful vegetable oil (preferably an oil with
  a nutty flavour such as sesame, soya or sunflower)
2 oz (55g) polyunsaturated margarine
2 tablespoonsful honey

1. Combine the rolled oats, oatmeal, wheatgerm and sea salt in a mixing bowl. Incorporate the dried pineapple, dried papaya, coconut flakes, banana chips, ground almonds, flaked almonds and raw cane sugar.

2. Stir the vegetable oil into the dry ingredients.

46

3. Melt the margarine and honey together in a saucepan set over a moderate heat, then pour into the mixing bowl, blending well to bind the oats and other ingredients together.

4. Press the mixture evenly into a greased Swiss- roll tin measuring 9×13 in. (23×33cm), smoothing over with a palette knife and making sure that the mixture is well compressed.

5. Bake at 350°F/180°C (Gas Mark 4) for about 30 minutes, until nicely browned on top.

6. Allow to cool slightly after removing from the oven, then carefully cut into bars, but leave to cool thoroughly before removing from the baking tin.

Cuts into 18 bars.

ORANGE YOGURT FINGERS

Fresh orange juice, orange zest, natural yogurt and almonds are combined to make these deliciously fruity fingers.

½ lb (225g) wholemeal flour
2 oz (55g) ground almonds
½ level teaspoonful bicarbonate of soda
2 oranges
4 oz (115g) polyunsaturated margarine
4 oz (115g) raw cane sugar
2 oz (55g) nibbed almonds
1-2 tablespoonful natural yogurt
Lightly beaten egg white, to glaze

For decoration:

Split blanched almonds
Clear honey

1. Place the wholemeal flour, ground almonds and bicarbonate of soda in a mixing bowl. Finely grate the zest from the oranges into the mixing bowl.

2. Rub the margarine into the zest-flavoured dry ingredients, until the mixture resembles fine breadcrumbs. Now stir in the raw cane sugar and nibbed almonds.

3. Extract the juice from one of the oranges and stir into the flour mixture, together with sufficient natural

yogurt to bind the ingredients to a stiff, but fairly sticky dough.

4. Press the mixture into a greased Swiss-roll tin measuring 9 × 13 in. (23 × 33 cm). Brush all over with lightly beaten egg white, to glaze the surface.

5. Bake at 350°F/180°C (Gas Mark 4) for 20 minutes, then reduce the oven temperature to 325°F/160°C (Gas Mark 3), and bake for a further 10-12 minutes, until golden brown and firm to the touch.

6. When thoroughly cool, cut into finger-sized biscuits and decorate with some split blanched almonds, secured with a little clear honey.

Cuts into 30 fingers.

MUESLI SLICES

Packed with the goodness of mixed grains, dried fruits and nuts, these delicious fibre-rich slices are a real family favourite.

4 oz (115g) unsweetened mixed grain muesli base
4 oz (115g) wholemeal flour
1 oz (30g) wheatgerm
½ level teaspoonful bicarbonate of soda
5 oz (140g) polyunsaturated margarine
4 oz (115g) light Muscovado sugar
2 oz (55g) nibbed almonds
1 oz (30g) sultanas
1 oz (30g) raisins
1 oz (30g) dried pineapple, finely diced
1 oz (30g) dried apricots, finely diced
½ teaspoonful vanilla essence
1 egg, lightly beaten
2 teaspoonsful clear honey
4-5 tablespoonsful milk
Lightly beaten egg white, to glaze

1. Combine the muesli base, wholemeal flour, wheatgerm and bicarbonate of soda in a mixing bowl.

2. Using the fingertips, rub the margarine into the dry ingredients.

3. Fold in the Muscovado sugar, almonds, sultanas, raisins, pineapple, apricots and vanilla essence.

4. Now incorporate the beaten egg and honey, together with sufficient milk to bind the ingredients to a fairly stiff consistency.

5. Press the mixture evenly into a greased Swiss-roll tin measuring 9×13 in. (23×33cm) smoothing over with a palette knife and making sure that the mixture is well compressed.

6. Brush all over with lightly beaten egg white, to glaze, then bake at 350°F/180°C (Gas Mark 4) for 25-30 minutes, until nicely browned and firm to the touch.

7. Allow to cool slightly after removing from the oven, then carefully cut into slices, but leave to cool thoroughly before removing from the baking tin.

Cuts into 18 slices.

APPLE AND COCONUT FINGERS

The natural flavour of fresh apples is contained in these coconut and honey topped fingers.

> 10 oz (285g) wholemeal flour
> 1 level teaspoonful bicarbonate of soda
> 4 oz (115g) polyunsaturated margarine
> 4 oz (115g) raw cane sugar
> 1 lb (455g) dessert apples (Golden Delicious or
>   similar)
> Finely grated zest of 1 lemon
> 2 teaspoonsful clear honey
> 2 tablespoonsful natural yogurt
> Lightly beaten egg white, to glaze

For topping:

> Clear honey
> 1½ oz (40g) desiccated coconut

1. Place the wholemeal flour and bicarbonate of soda in a mixing bowl.

2. Rub the margarine into the dry ingredients, until the mixture resembles fine breadcrumbs. Now incorporate the raw cane sugar.

3. Peel and core the apples, then coarsely grate into the flour mixture.

4. Add the finely grated lemon zest and honey, then bind

the ingredients together with the natural yogurt.

5. Press the mixture evenly into a greased Swiss-roll tin measuring 9 × 13 in. (23 × 33cm) then brush all over with lightly beaten egg white, to glaze the surface.

6. Bake at 350°F/180°C (Gas Mark 4) for 25-30 minutes, until golden brown and firm to the touch.

7. Allow to cool in the baking tin, then cut into finger shapes. Coat the topside of the fingers with some clear honey, then sprinkle with desiccated coconut.

Cuts into 30 fingers.

CAROB AND PECAN SQUARES

Dark and delicious, rich in the flavour of carob, pecans and honey.

3 oz (85g) wholemeal flour
1 oz (30g) carob powder
1 level teaspoonful bicarbonate of soda
4 oz (115g) polyunsaturated margarine
2 generous tablespoonsful honey
2 eggs, lightly beaten
½ teaspoonful vanilla essence
2 oz (55g) chopped pecans

For decoration:

16 whole pecans
Clear honey

1. Combine the wholemeal flour, carob powder and bicarbonate of soda in a mixing bowl.

2. Melt the margarine and honey together in a saucepan set over a moderate heat.

3. Add the beaten eggs, melted margarine and honey and vanilla essence to the dry ingredients, beating well until smooth and thoroughly blended. Now fold in the chopped pecans.

4. Pour the mixture into a greased 8 in. (20cm) square, shallow baking tin, and bake at 350°F/180°C (Gas

Mark 4) for about 20 minutes. The mixture will begin to shrink from the sides of the baking tin when ready.

5.   Allow to cool in the baking tin, then cut into squares. Coat the underside of the whole pecans with a little clear honey and place one on each of the squares, to decorate.

Cuts into 16 small squares.

CLIVE BIRCH

SUNFLOWER SEED AND APPLE SLICES

A wealth of natural ingredients that includes protein-rich sunflower seeds, dried fruits and oatmeal is contained in these flavourful slices.

½ lb (225g) wholemeal flour
2 oz (55g) fine oatmeal
2 level teaspoonsful ground cinnamon
½ level teaspoonful ground nutmeg
1 level teaspoonful bicarbonate of soda
4 oz (115g) polyunsaturated margarine
3 oz (85g) raw cane sugar
2 oz (55g) sunflower seeds
2 oz (55g) dried apple rings, finely diced
1 oz (30g) sultanas
1 tablespoonful clear honey
1 egg, lightly beaten
1-2 tablespoonsful milk
Lightly beaten egg white, to glaze

1. Place the wholemeal flour, oatmeal, spices and bicarbonate of soda in a mixing bowl. Using the fingertips, rub the margarine into the dry ingredients until the mixture resembles fine breadcrumbs.

2. Stir in the raw cane sugar, sunflower seeds, diced apple rings and sultanas.

3. Incorporate the clear honey, blending well. Now add the beaten egg, together with sufficient milk to bind

the ingredients to a fairly stiff dough.

4. Press the mixture into a greased Swiss-roll tin measuring 9 × 13 in. (23 × 33cm) then brush all over with lightly beaten egg white, to glaze the surface.

5. Bake at 350°F/180°C (Gas Mark 4) for 20-25 minutes, until golden brown and firm to the touch.

6. Allow to cool thoroughly, then cut into slices.

Cuts into 18 slices.

C L I V E   B I R C H

PEAR, HONEY AND ALMOND SLICES

This combination of fresh pears, honey and almonds, subtly flavoured with lemon zest, is as delicious as it is nutritious.

10 oz (285g) wholemeal flour
2 oz (55g) ground almonds
1 level teaspoonful bicarbonate of soda
2 pears, peeled, cored and finely diced
3 oz (85g) nibbed almonds
Finely grated zest of 2 lemons
4 oz (115g) polyunsaturated margarine
3 tablespoonsful honey
Lightly beaten egg white, to glaze

For decoration:

Split blanched almonds
Clear honey

1. Combine the wholemeal flour, ground almonds and bicarbonate of soda in a mixing bowl.

2. Add the diced pears, nibbed almonds and finely grated lemon zest to the dry ingredients.

3. Melt the margarine and honey together in a saucepan set over a moderate heat. Pour the melted margarine and honey into the mixing bowl, binding the ingredients to a fairly stiff dough.

4. Press the mixture evenly into a greased Swiss-roll tin

measuring 9 × 13 in. (23 × 33cm) then brush all over with lightly beaten egg white, to glaze the surface.

5. Bake at 350°F/180°C (Gas Mark 4) for 25-30 minutes, until golden brown and firm to the touch. Allow to cool in the baking tin, then cut into slices.

6. Decorate the slices with some split blanched almonds, secured with a little clear honey.

Cuts into 18 slices.

RAISIN AND MOLASSES FINGERS

Two concentrated sources of natural sugars, raisins and molasses, are harmoniously combined in these dark and spicy fingers.

½ lb (225g) wholemeal flour
2 oz (55g) fine oatmeal
2 level teaspoonsful ground cinnamon
½ level teaspoonful ground nutmeg
1 level teaspoonful bicarbonate of soda
4 oz (115g) small raisins, diced
3 oz (85g) polyunsaturated margarine
2 tablespoonsful blackstrap molasses
1 tablespoonful natural yogurt
Lightly beaten egg white, to glaze

For decoration:

Split blanched almonds
Clear honey

1. Combine the wholemeal flour, oatmeal, spices and bicarbonate of soda in a mixing bowl. Add the raisins to the dry ingredients.

2. Melt the margarine and molasses together in a saucepan set over a moderate heat. Stir the melted margarine and molasses into the dry ingredients, blending thoroughly, then incorporate the natural yogurt.

3. Press the mixture evenly into a greased Swiss-roll tin measuring 9 × 13 in. (23 × 33cm) then brush all over with lightly beaten egg white.

4. Bake at 350°F/180°C (Gas Mark 4) for about 20 minutes, until firm to the touch.

5. Allow to cool thoroughly in the baking tin, then cut into fingers. Decorate the fingers with some split blanched almonds, secured with a little clear honey.

Cuts into 30 fingers.

HONEY FLAPJACKS

Oats, honey and cinnamon are combined to make this version of the classic flapjack.

½ lb (225g) porridge oats
1½ level teaspoonsful ground cinnamon
3 oz (85g) light Muscovado sugar
5 oz (140g) polyunsaturated margarine
1 tablespoonful honey

1. Combine the oats, cinnamon and Muscovado sugar in a mixing bowl.

2. Melt the margarine and honey together in a saucepan set over a moderate heat.

3. Stir the melted margarine and honey into the oat mixture, mixing well to bind the oats together.

4. Press the mixture evenly into a greased 8 in. (20cm) square shallow baking tin, smoothing over with the back of a tablespoon and making sure that the mixture is well compressed.

5. Bake at 350°F/180°C (Gas Mark 4) for 20-25 minutes, until golden brown.

6. Allow to cool slightly after removing from the oven, then carefully cut into squares, but leave to cool thoroughly before removing from the baking tin.

Cuts into 12 pieces.

INDEX